Bernard Caldwell

MAKE YOUR TIME WORK:Focus on What Truly Matters Each Day.

To those who are constantly looking for the truth and enlightenment, the curious minds. This book is dedicated to you, the persistent investigators of reality, who dared to probe the limits of human comprehension. May the wisdom found inside these pages act as a compass, leading you on an illuminating journey, and help you to create a better future.

Contents

1.

2.

1.

Acknowledgement

I want to sincerely thank everyone who has helped me along the way while I've been writing this book. This job would not have been accomplished without their support, direction, and unfailing faith in me.

I owe a huge debt of gratitude to my family for their unfailing love and support. They helped me tremendously over the many hours I spent writing this book by being kind and patient.

I want to express my sincere gratitude to my editor, whose knowledge and helpful criticism greatly enhanced the quality of this paper. Your meticulous attention to detail and commitment to improving my work have been simply amazing.

I'm appreciative to all the people who so kindly imparted their wisdom and experiences to me. Your opinions and insights have enriched and expanded upon this book.

I would like to express my gratitude for the support of my research associates and the experts who shared their knowledge and skills in the domains in which they work. Your contributions have significantly improved this book's accuracy and breadth of content.

I owe a debt of gratitude to my friends and coworkers for their unwavering encouragement and support. Your kind feedback and confidence in my abilities have served as a regular source of motivation.

Finally, I'd want to thank the readers for coming along on this literary adventure with me. The greatest reward for my efforts is to see your interest in and involvement with this book.

I want to thank you all for taking part in this amazing project. This book has been eternally changed by your efforts, no matter how large or small, and I will always be grateful for having had you in my life.

1

Introduction

1. There is no so Much Time

There are moments when it seems like time is slipping through our fingers like sand in the rush and bustle of modern life. Even though each day is made up of the same 24 hours, it seems like there is never enough time to do everything we want to do. The shortage of time is a daily problem we all face, regardless of whether it's personal aspirations, professional ambitions, or simply finding time for enjoyment and leisure.

Although time is a precious and irreplaceable resource, it is also always passing. We are coming closer to the end with each passing second, which serves as a depressing reminder of how short our time is. This sobering thought forces us to think carefully about how we choose to spend our limited time. We frequently hear recommendations to maximize our time, seize the day, and fully experience life. But the question still stands: Why do we regularly feel as though we are running out of time?

2. Our Time is Primarily Absorbed by Default

While it is true that we have a finite amount of time, it is equally true that much of it is spent automatically, without conscious thought or intent. In the current society, we have created daily routines and rituals that suck up major chunks of our waking hours. Our lives are frequently dominated from the moment we get up until the moment we go to bed by commitments, responsibilities, and outside expectations.

Many people in the industry are locked in a vicious cycle of long hours, demanding deadlines, and continuous pressure to perform well. The pursuit of achievement typically comes at the sacrifice of time, whether it be in the shape of a challenging task, a company operation, or an intellectual effort. Our schedules fill up rapidly with meetings, projects, and to-do lists, leaving little time for personal reflection or pursuing other hobbies.

Technology has a big impact on how we manage our time outside of the workplace. Social media sites, streaming services, and appealing smartphone apps have matured into pervasive distractions that catch our interest and fill our leisure time. We may easily waste hours of our day incessantly scrolling through newsfeeds, binge-watching entire seasons of television series, and participating in online forums.

In addition, executing daily duties like errands, household chores, and transportation take up a large chunk of our time. These necessary but usually laborious jobs could appear like time vampires that drain our energy and leave us with little ability for other fun pursuits.

It is vital to pause in this scenario and give our time some serious thought. Are we using it in ways that are consistent with our beliefs, ambitions, and ongoing development as individuals? Are we using our time wisely, or are we just going through the motions and letting the days pass us by?

The first step in recovering control over our lives is comprehending how precious time is and the natural tendencies that savor it. It requires making a conscious effort to look at our routines, identify time wasters, and find constructive ways to spend our days. Setting limits, prioritizing our objectives, and acquiring the ability to turn down activities that clash with our ideals or improve our welfare are a few examples of how to do this.

Finally, in our fast-paced existence, time is a vital and scarce resource that frequently eludes us. But a considerable percentage of our time is spent mechanically, without deliberate thought or effort. We must sit back, review our routines and habits, and intentionally decide how we want to spend our days if we are to make the most of our time. By doing this, we may fight the ingrained behaviors that restrict our time and construct a life that is more rewarding, meaningful, and in keeping with our true aspirations.

2

HOW TO MAKE YOUR TIME WORK

• That is achieved by following these four basic steps:

1. Spotlight:Begin Your Day By Selecting a Central Focus

Your productivity and general well-being can be considerably increased by beginning the day with intention and attention. Embracing the idea of "spotlighting"—deciding on a primary focus or objective for the day—is one efficient way to do this. Here's a brief guide on how to choose your day's main topic in the morning:

a.Clarity is key. Before you start your day, think about your long-term objectives and desires. Knowing what is most important to you will enable you to choose a central focus that is consistent with your priorities and values.

Prioritize your work by focusing on the most important tasks or goals. Think about each task's necessity, significance, and potential effects. Choose one main goal from this list that you wish to focus all of your attention and resources on for the day.

b.One thing at a time: Avoid overextending yourself by attempting to handle several priorities at once. Instead, commit to giving your full concentration to the principal focus you've picked. With this strategy, you may focus your efforts on making significant advancements.

c.Maintain flexibility: It's critical to be adaptive while maintaining a strong focus. Recognize that unexpected events or fresh possibilities can occur during the day. Examine their applicability and, if required, shift your attention, but make an effort to stay on course.

Take time to recognize and celebrate your accomplishments as you move closer to your primary goal. Recognizing your efforts will increase motivation and strengthen the practice of starting the day with a focused intention.

2. Beam: Overcome Distractions to Carve out Time For Your Spotlight

It's crucial to set up a space that allows you to maintain attention and reduce distractions once you've selected the main topic for your day through spotlighting. Here, the idea of "beaming"—directing your focus and energy into your spotlight—comes into play. Here is some succinct advice on how to put aside time for your spotlight and ignore distractions:

a.Determine distractions: To begin, determine the typical sources of attention-diversion and productivity-robbing distractions. Social media, email notifications, excessive noise, or interruptions from coworkers or family members could all be contributing factors. The first step in combating these distractions is to recognize them.

b.Set boundaries: To safeguard your time and attention, establish firm boundaries. In both your personal and professional life, let others know that you are focused and available. Tell them that you appreciate minimum interruptions during your set apart times for uninterrupted work or reflection.

c.Establish a dedicated workspace: Pick a location where you may work or perform tasks connected to your spotlight. This could be a distinct space, a serene nook, or even a particular desk. Make sure this area is free from unneeded interruptions and equipped with whatever you need to be focused on.

Digital distractions are common in today's linked society, so practice digital restraint. By disabling notifications on your devices, using website blockers or time management apps, and scheduling certain times for checking emails or using social media, you can take proactive measures to reduce them. Instead of letting technology take control of your attention, use it as a tool to support your focus.

Blocking your time will allow you to devote specific periods to working on your spotlight. Consider these pieces of time as binding promises to yourself. During these times, refrain from multitasking and focus entirely on the task at hand. To stay focused and prevent getting overwhelmed, divide larger jobs into more manageable, smaller pieces.

Develop mindfulness practices to help you focus on your focus again when you see yourself becoming distracted by other things. To refresh your mind and recover attention, schedule regular breaks for deep breathing, meditation, or quick physical activity. Develop self-awareness to spot when your focus begins to wander and intentionally refocus it on your main objective.

3. Energize:Harness the Body's Energy to Rejuvenate the Mind

We frequently feel as though we cannot keep up with the incessant demands of technology, employment, and responsibilities. But what if I told you that by utilizing the strength of your body's energy, you could revitalize and make the most of your time? It is real! We may discover the secret to refreshing our thoughts and making the most of our time by comprehending the relationship between our bodies and minds.

Prioritizing rest and healing is one essential component. We frequently undervalue the value of obtaining enough sleep. We can boost our cognitive function and increase our overall productivity by developing a regular sleep schedule and making sure we get enough rest. A relaxed mind is a focused mind.

Maintaining energy levels and mental clarity also depends on feeding our bodies the proper nutrients. A well-rounded diet that includes whole foods, lean proteins, healthy fats, and complex carbohydrates gives you the nutrition you need for all-day energy. Avoiding excessive amounts of sugar, caffeine, and processed foods helps us stay alert and productive by preventing energy collapses.

The benefits of physical activity extend to our mental health as well as our physical health. Regular exercise improves blood flow to the brain, which releases neurotransmitters and endorphins that elevate mood, lower stress levels, and enhance cognitive performance. Stretching or taking a little stroll can both reenergize our minds and boost productivity in even brief periods of physical exercise.

It's simple to get lost in the craziness of our fast-paced lives and forget to be in the moment. Mindfulness and meditation can help with it. Stress may be reduced, mental clarity can be improved, and decision-making abilities can be strengthened by setting aside some time each day to calm our minds, concentrate on the here and now, and practice deep breathing.

4. Reflect:Refine and Enhance Your System

• **Assess Your Current System:** Reflect begins by inviting you to assess your current time management system. It prompts you to review your everyday routines, workflows, and procedures. By taking a step back and critically assessing your system, you obtain a clearer knowledge of its strengths and flaws. Reflect allows you to identify areas that demand improvement, such as excessive multitasking, lack of priority, or ineffective communication channels.

• **Identify and Eliminate Time**-Wasting Activities: One of the key purposes of Reflect is to help you identify time-wasting activities and eliminate them from your routine. The application allows you to think about your everyday tasks and evaluate their value and impact on your goals. By recognizing and removing non-essential activities or those that contribute little to your productivity, you free up important time and mental energy. Reflect helps you to focus on tasks that genuinely matter, enabling you to do more in less time.

•**Adapt and Prioritize:** Reflect and recognizes the dynamic nature of our lives and work. It pushes you to modify your time management approach to changing conditions and priorities. By constantly reflecting on your goals, Reflect helps you reassess and reprioritize work properly. The application provides a platform for evaluating the urgency and importance of each activity, allowing you to make informed decisions about where to devote your time and resources. With Reflect, you can stay adaptable and ensure your efforts fit with your shifting objectives.

• **Track and Analyze Time Allocation** To make time work for you, it's vital to understand how you manage your time. Reflect offers powerful time tracking and analysis functions, enabling you to obtain insights into your time use trends. By documenting your activities and classifying them, the program provides statistics and visualizations that show how you spend your time. Reflect's analytics equip you to detect patterns of inefficiency, potential distractions, and time gaps that can be better utilized. This knowledge allows you to make data-driven decisions and optimize your time allocation.

•**Cultivate Mindfulness and Attention**: Reflect Spotlights the significance of mindfulness and attention inefficient time management. The application encourages you to add thoughtful practices to your routine, such as meditation or brief moments of reflection throughout the day. Reflect also helps you reduce distractions by defining boundaries, generating specific intervals of uninterrupted work, and employing strategies like the Pomodoro Technique. By increasing mindfulness and limiting distractions, Reflect helps your capacity to stay focused and execute activities efficiently.

•**Continuous Improvement**: Reflect realizes that time management is an ongoing process of refinement and improvement. It encourages a mindset of constant learning and growth. The tool prompts you to routinely evaluate and reassess your system, exploring chances for further improvement. Reflect encourages you to experiment with various methods, tools, and techniques, empowering you to uncover what works best for you. By embracing a culture of continual development, Reflect enables you to enhance your productivity and make time work in your favor.

3

SPOTLIGHT

•The lost Months

Sometimes, we may feel as if time is passing so quickly, and we haven't accomplished or experienced much. This sensation often originates from a lack of awareness and appreciation for the Spotlights in our life. We may overlook or downplay significant moments, allowing chunks of time to feel like they have been "lost" or unremarkable. By deliberately seeking out and acknowledging the Spotlights, we may fill these gaps and create a more fulfilling perception of time.

•What will be the of Your Day?

Each day brings opportunity for remarkable experiences, achievements, or moments of joy. The Spotlight of your day refers to the event or experience that stands out as the most important, thrilling, or noteworthy. It could be anything as little as a kind gesture from a stranger, a breakthrough in a personal project, or a moment of connection with a loved one. By finding the Spotlight, you can ponder on it, appreciate the wonderful emotions associated with it, and generate a sense of fulfillment.

•Three Ways to Choose Your Spotlight

a. **Reflect on your emotions**: Consider the instances that elicited the strongest positive emotions or provided you the most happiness, fulfillment, or contentment. Emotions often act as markers of noteworthy experiences.

a. **Identify your goals and values:** Reflect on your priorities and the goals you have set for yourself. Evaluate whatever moments or activities from your day correspond with these goals and beliefs. The progress you make towards your goals or the activities that resonate with your values might serve as significant Spotlights.

c. **Consider long-term impact**: Think about the moments that have the potential for long-lasting consequences on your life. These could be experiences that contribute to personal growth, extend your horizons, or build significant friendships. Such moments, even though apparently insignificant at the time, can carry great value in molding your journey.

•Trust your nerve to Choose the Ideal Spotlight

While soliciting opinion from others can be beneficial, it is equally crucial to trust your instincts and intuition when choosing a Spotlight. Your gut sense can direct you toward recognizing the moments that truly resonate with you on a personal level. It helps you to connect into your own emotions, tastes, and values, ultimately resulting to a more real and meaningful selection of Spotlights.

•Spotlight strategies

1.Select your Spotlight

Actively select the Spotlight of your day or a specified time frame. By actively making this choice, you prioritize what actually matters to you and concentrate your attention and energy towards it. This exercise helps you focus on the positive features and crucial events, boosting your whole experience.

2.Jot it Down

Documenting your chosen Spotlight is a strong approach to solidify its value. By writing it down, you establish a concrete record that you can reread later. This exercise also helps in establishing a collection of unforgettable memories, giving a valuable resource for contemplation and thankfulness.

3.Repeat Yesterday Again

This approach entails recreating or re-creating a very delightful or productive day. Reflect on a former day that stands out as a Spotlight and identify the components that made it unique. Then, try to incorporate such elements into your present or future days. This strategy allows you to revisit the wonderful experience and optimize your present routines for better fulfillment.

4.Establish a Hierarchy for Your Life

Prioritize and rate the different parts of your life according on their relevance and impact. By recognizing your personal beliefs and what actually important to you, you can manage your time and energy accordingly. This strategy helps you make intentional choices, ensuring that your time is spent on activities and experiences that correspond with your values.

5.Bundle the Small Stuff

Minimize distractions and boost efficiency by grouping comparable or routine jobs together. Instead of addressing little, mundane activities individually throughout the day, set up certain time blocks to tackle them in batches. This strategy allows you to free up more time and mental space for significant activities and Spotlights.

6.The Could-Do List

Instead of overwhelming oneself with a large to-do list, develop a Could-do list. This list comprises of a few high-priority tasks or activities that have the potential to become Spotlights. By focusing on a shorter list, you may spend your resources more effectively and increase the likelihood of having important experiences.

7.The On-Hold List

The On-Hold List is a productivity technique devised by the developer of the "Productivity System for Creative People." It entails scribbling down everything that distracts or occupies your thoughts. By collecting these thoughts and chores, you can reduce mental clutter, letting you to focus on your chosen Spotlight and vital activities.

8.Undertake an Individual Sprint

An Individual sprint is a focused and intense burst of effort geared to attaining a specific goal or objective. Set aside a specific period of time, such as a day or a week, to concentrate on making considerable improvement in a certain area. By focusing your energy into a sprint, you can increase productivity and create a Spotlight of success.

4

BEAM

• Why infinity pools are so difficult to keep from

The concept of infinity pools refers to undertakings or activities that have no obvious goal or that might easily absorb excessive amounts of time. These tasks often include scrolling through social media, binge-watching TV series, or getting caught up in constant online browsing. They are seductive and hard to refuse since they deliver rapid gratification and can be immensely entertaining. However, yielding to infinity pools can be counterproductive to time maximizing. Recognizing these distractions and deliberately regulating your engagement with them is vital to prevent squandering precious time.

•Take Control of Your Time Without Relying on Technology

Technology developments have the potential to enhance productivity and save time, but relying only on technology to manage your time can be counterproductive. Instead of waiting for technical solutions to miraculously give you back time, take an active role in managing your time wisely. Set clear goals, define priorities, and build tactics to avoid distractions and enhance your productivity. Remember that you have the authority to make conscious choices and maximize your time, regardless of the available technologies.

•Create Obstacles For Distractions

Distractions can severely impair time maximization efforts. To resist distractions, it's vital to develop boundaries that minimize their influence on your focus and productivity. Here are a few tactics to consider:

a. Remove physical distractions

Minimize clutter and create an ordered environment that improves attention. Keep your mobile devices out of sight or utilize programs that limit access to distracting websites or applications during focused work periods.

b. Establish time boundaries

Set specific periods for focused work or deep concentration without interruptions. Communicate these boundaries to colleagues, family members, or roommates, ensuring they respect your assigned time for productive work.

c. Practice mindful task-switching

Multitasking can be detrimental, resulting in diminished focus and increased time spent on each task. Instead, focus on one activity at a time, complete it, or reach a certain milestone before moving on to the next one. This helps maintain momentum and reduces the time lost due to frequent context switching.

d. Utilize productivity tactics

Explore time-management techniques like the Pomodoro Technique, where you work in focused sprints with brief pauses in between. These approaches can boost your concentration and productivity by bringing structure and rhythm to your work.

•Beam strategies

a.Take Control of your phone

Take charge of your phone usage by being attentive to how you engage with it. Set boundaries and develop guidelines for yourself regarding phone usage. Be mindful about when and how you use your phone, and avoid getting trapped in mindless scrolling or excessive app usage. By becoming the ruler of your phone, you can avoid it from being a source of distraction and time-wasting.

b.Try a Phone Without the distraction

Consider using a distraction-free phone or a simpler device that focuses primarily on critical functions like calls, messages, and vital apps. These gadgets frequently lack social media apps or other time-consuming features, helping you stay focused and limit distractions. By embracing a distraction-free phone, you can boost your productivity and maintain better control over your time.

c.Sign Out

When utilizing online platforms or applications, make it a practice to sign out when you're done. Logging out adds an extra step and makes it less easy to access these platforms impulsively. It functions as an intentional barrier, allowing you a chance to reconsider before mindlessly connecting with them. By logging out, you establish a pause that allows you to reassess and maybe dedicate your time to more meaningful pursuits.

d.Stop notifications

Assess and limit the notifications you receive on your phone or other devices. Notifications can be a constant source of interruptions and distractions, diverting your attention away from vital work. Disable or modify notifications to lessen their impact on your focus. By decreasing the number of notifications, you may recover control over your attention and allocate your time more strategically.

e.Clear your home screen

Arrange your phone's home screen to be clutter-free and orderly. Remove unneeded apps or widgets that may encourage you to spend time or distract you. Keep only the important apps exposed and easily accessible. A clean home screen avoids visual distractions and lets you focus on the tasks or programs that are genuinely important.

f.Put a watch on

Consider wearing a wristwatch as a time management tool. Having a watch on your wrist gives you a convenient way to check the time without relying on your phone. By decreasing the need to reach for your phone only to check the time, you prevent getting sidetracked by other apps or notifications that may tempt you. A wristwatch helps you stay focused and aware of time throughout the day.

•SLOW YOUR INBOX

Take a purposeful and concentrated approach to managing your inbox when dealing with emails. Instead of checking and replying to emails throughout the day, schedule a certain time to process them. Email jobs can be batch-processed to reduce interruptions and increase efficiency.

a.Plan your email time

Schedule certain periods each day or each week for handling emails. Put all of your attention towards processing and answering emails within these set times. With this method, you can better manage your time and stop emails from taking over your entire day.

Try to reach inbox 0 at least once every week by clearing your inbox. Make sure your inbox is clean and only contains things you can act on by taking the time to sift, reply, and organize your emails. Regularly cleaning up your email will make you feel accomplished and lessen the stress that comes with having a cluttered inbox.

b.Pretend that messages are letters

Instead of treating incoming messages as urgent tasks, treat them as "letters". Resist the need to reply to every email that comes in right away. As an alternative, order your chores by importance and deal with the most urgent ones first. You may keep your attention on higher-priority tasks by changing your perspective and treating emails as less urgent tasks.

c.Take your time answering emails

Not all of them require a prompt response. Permit yourself to react more slowly unless it is urgent or important. Establish realistic expectations with other people regarding your response timings, and try not to feel rushed to answer right away. Being thoughtful in your responses can help you manage your time more effectively and spend less time in your email.

• IDENTIFY FLOW

a.Close the door

Establish a boundary, whether it be physical or mental, to reduce interruptions and distractions. Find a place that is peaceful and alone so you can focus on your work without interruptions from the outside world. By doing so, you may be able to achieve a state of flow where your attention is completely on the activity at hand, maximizing your productivity and efficiency.

b.Create your deadlines

Set internal deadlines even in the absence of external ones. Setting specific time limits for your projects helps you to establish a sense of urgency that might improve your motivation and focus. These deadlines provide your work structure and aid in prioritizing it, allowing you to finish chores more quickly.

c.Use a countdown clock or visible timer

You can maintain awareness of how much time you have left for a specific work by having a visual reminder of time passing. This aids in maintaining attention and can help you avoid getting sidetracked by pointless pursuits.

d.Refuse to be Tricked to use Fancy Tools

Although productivity tools might be useful, you should take care not to get sucked into testing out new hardware or software that claims to increase your productivity. Use tools that are compatible with your workflow and that you are already familiar with to concentrate on the task at hand. Your time and productivity should be maximized, not lost in the novelty of new technologies.

You may make the most of your time and achieve a state of intense focus and productivity by using these flow-finding techniques. Remember that achieving flow entails creating a focused environment, establishing specific goals and deadlines, and eliminating pointless interruptions. Prioritize your work based on its significance and influence while embracing simplicity.

5

ENERGIZE

•You are Bigger Than a Brain

Recognize that you are more than just a brain and that your physical and emotional health are not simply influenced by your mental health. Maintaining your physical health, emotional stability, and social relationships is crucial. To keep your energy levels high and increase your productivity, take part in activities that are good for your body, mind, and spirit.

•The Contemporary Way of Living is Accidental.

Recognize that the pace and demands of the modern lifestyle can be strenuous and draining. Your energy can be depleted by a variety of characteristics of modern living, including continual connectedness, information overload, and sedentary work settings. Be mindful of these issues and take the initiative to balance them.

•Act Like a Caveman to increase Energy

Adopt lifestyle habits modeled after those of our ancestors to increase energy. This comprises:

a. **Make sleep a priority.** You need enough good sleep to recharge your batteries. To encourage the best possible rest, establish a regular sleep schedule and provide a sleep-friendly environment.

b. Move your body: Exercise frequently to improve stamina, increase blood flow, and boost general energy levels. Make time for activities you enjoy and incorporate them into your schedule.

c. Consume nutritious meals: To provide your body with the nutrition it needs, eat a balanced diet that includes whole, unprocessed foods. Give high priority to nutrients like complex carbs, lean proteins, and healthy fats that deliver long-lasting energy.

d. Manage your stress well: Prolonged tension can drain your energy. To lower stress levels and refuel your energy, incorporate stress-reduction strategies like mindfulness, meditation, deep breathing, or indulging in hobbies.

e. Encourage social connections: Engaging in meaningful social interactions and quality time with loved ones will lift your spirits and give you more energy. Develop connections with people who are supportive, connecting, and upbeat.

f. Allow yourself to take regular pauses throughout the day to rest and refuel. Taking a break from work or mentally taxing activities might help you regain focus and energy.

You can invigorate yourself and make the most of your time by realizing that you are more than your intellect, comprehending the effects of the modern lifestyle, and embracing techniques derived from our ancestors. Remember that maintaining your physical and mental health is essential for having prolonged energy and working at your best.

Energize strategies

a.Exercise regularly

Make exercise a daily ritual. Exercise results in the release of endorphins, a decrease in tension, and an improvement in endurance. Find hobbies you like, whether it's playing team sports, doing yoga, or going on a run. Put consistency first, and make exercising a mandatory component of your day.

b.pounding the pavement

Take advantage of the stimulating effects of walking or running outside by. Spend time in nature and discover your surroundings rather than only exercising indoors. Your mind and body can be revitalized by the fresh air, sunlight, and change of scenery, which will naturally give you more energy.

c.Self-inflicted inconveniences

This be intentionally incorporated into a daily schedule to encourage exercise and raise energy expenditure. Take the stairs instead of the elevator, park further away from your destination, or opt to walk or ride a bike for quick errands. These irritations might seem insignificant, but they add up and help to promote an active and energizing lifestyle.

d.Fit in a super-heated workout

When time is short, use short yet intensive workouts that will instantly increase your heart rate and give you more energy. Workouts involving circuit training or high-intensity interval training (HIIT) are both terrific choices. These routines maximize your workout's efficiency in the least amount of time possible by alternating brief bursts of intensive exercise with rest periods.

Making the most of your time and boosting your overall energy levels can be accomplished by including these energizing strategies in your everyday routine. Regular exercise, especially outside, can enhance your physical and emotional well-being and provide you with a sustained energy boost. To maintain an active and energizing lifestyle, keep consistency as your top priority and choose activities you enjoy.

EAT AUTHENTIC FOOD

a.Eat Well

Adopt a whole-foods-based, nutrient-dense diet that emulates our predecessors' eating habits. Give natural, unprocessed foods like fruits, vegetables, lean meats, fish, nuts, and seeds a high priority. Reduce your intake of artificial additives, refined sugars, and processed meals. You may improve your energy levels, focus, and general well-being by feeding your body actual, healthy foods.

b.Fill your plate with necessary food

Fill at least half of your plate with a range of vibrant fruits and vegetables to make plants the focal point of your meals. Essential vitamins, minerals, fiber, and antioxidants are present in these plant-based foods, supporting optimum health and energy levels. To make a balanced and delicious dinner, pair them with high-quality protein sources and healthy fats.

Follow your body's indications for hunger and fullness to maintain your appetite. Eat just when you are hungry, and stop when you are comfortably full. Refrain from overeating or thoughtless nibbling while you're bored or feeling emotional. You may improve digestion, energy levels, and general well-being by establishing a healthy relationship with food and paying attention to your body's cues.

c.Snack Like A kid

Snack like a kid by picking entire, unadulterated foods that will provide you lasting energy and nourishment. Choose healthy snacks like yogurt with few additives, fresh fruits, and raw vegetables with hummus, almonds, and seeds. Avoid highly processed snacks that are full of artificial ingredients, harmful fats, and added sugars. Snacking like a toddler entails choosing straightforward, healthy items that will nourish your body and boost productivity.

d.Visit the Dark Chocolate Plan

Visit the dark chocolate diet plan and include dark chocolate in moderation in your diet. The beneficial antioxidants and chemicals found in dark chocolate with a high cocoa content (70 percent or more) help improve mood, concentration, and cardiovascular health. Enjoy a little piece of dark chocolate throughout the day as a treat or pick-me-up, but be careful with portion sizes and pick products with few added sugars.

You may energize your body, support ideal energy levels, and make the most of your time by embracing the concept of eating genuine food. Underline complete, unprocessed meals, consume a variety of fruits and vegetables, pay attention to your body's hunger signals, select wholesome snacks, and occasionally treat yourself to a small amount of dark chocolate. Never forget that eating actual food fuels your body, which in turn stimulates your productivity and general well-being.

MAXIMIZE CAFFEINE

e.Caffeinate your day when wake up

A natural wake-up practice should be used to begin your day before drinking caffeine. Before turning to caffeine for an energy boost, let your body naturally awaken and arouse your senses. You may create a more sustainable and natural energy rhythm by doing this throughout the day.

f.Caffeinate before you Sleep

Use caffeine in advance to avoid energy crashes rather than waiting until you're already feeling weary or exhausted. To keep your alertness and focus during periods when your energy levels normally decline, strategically time your caffeine intake, such as in the middle of the morning or early in the afternoon.

g.Take a caffeine nap: To get the most out of both, combine the power of caffeine with a quick snooze. Drink something caffeinated before going to sleep because it takes some time for caffeine to take effect. After that, nap for about 15 to 20 minutes. You'll get the rewards of caffeine's alertness as well as the rejuvenating effects of a nap when you wake up.

f.Consider Green Tea Routine

Consider including green tea in your coffee routine to help you stay alert. Along with other healthy ingredients like L-theanine, which fosters calm attention, green tea also contains caffeine. In comparison to other caffeinated beverages, it offers a softer, longer-lasting energy boost. Green tea can keep you focused and productive without giving you the jitters or crashes that are frequently brought on by other caffeine sources.

You can maximize the benefits of caffeine consumption to increase productivity and make the most of your time. Use caffeine wisely by avoiding energy crashes, taking caffeine naps to maximize its restorative effects, and contemplating green tea for a mellower, longer-lasting energy boost. Remember to keep an eye on your caffeine intake because everyone reacts differently to caffeine and too much can have unfavorable   effects.

6

REFLECT

•Make Adjustment Using Scientific Methods

Adopt a scientific strategy to improve your time management and productivity. Try out various tactics, methods, and instruments that have been demonstrated to be efficient by studies and research. Investigate productivity frameworks, such as the Eisenhower Matrix, time blocking, or the Pomodoro Technique, instance. Put these strategies into practice, assess how they affect your productivity, and then adjust your strategy in light of the findings.

•Keep a journal to record your progress

Keep a log of your actions, jobs, and tactics that you employ. Keep tabs on your development and review it frequently to spot trends, achievements, and potential improvement areas. You can keep a journal or use digital tools to record your experiences, evaluate your productivity, and make data-driven choices to improve your time management techniques.

•tiny changes can have a large impact

Be aware that making gradual, tiny changes to your routines and habits can result in significant gains in your productivity and time management. Decide on particular areas where you can make tiny adjustments, such as enhancing your morning routine, putting in place a reliable planning system, or quitting time-wasting activities. Concentrate on one thing at a time, make adjustments gradually, and watch how your productivity increases as a result.

You may adjust your strategy, make sure your activities are in line with your objectives, and continually improve how efficiently you manage your time by reflecting. You can improve your time management techniques and get noticeable results by adopting scientific approaches, keeping track of your progress through note-taking, and embracing incremental alterations. Never forget that reflection is a crucial tool for self-awareness and ongoing development, allowing you to optimize your strategy and utilize your time to the fullest.